★ IT'S MY STATE! ★
Puerto Rico

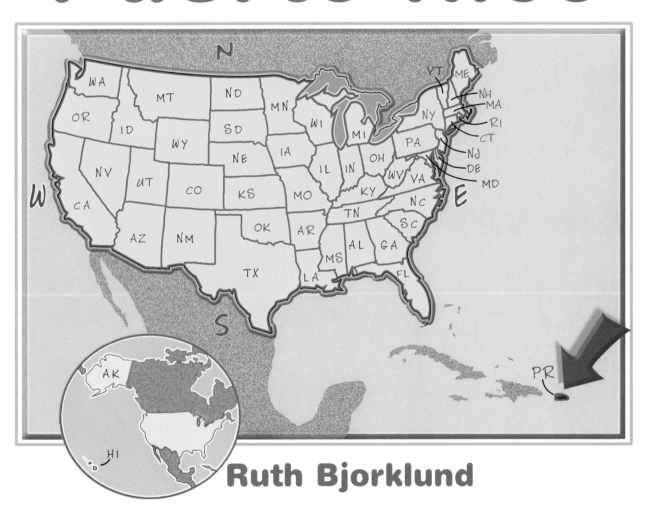

Ruth Bjorklund

Marshall Cavendish
Benchmark
New York

Marshall Cavendish Benchmark
99 White Plains Road
Tarrytown, New York 10591-9001
www.marshallcavendish.us

Library of Congress Cataloging-in-Publication Data

Bjorklund, Ruth.
Puerto Rico / by Ruth Bjorklund.
p. cm. -- (It's my state!)
Summary: "Surveys the history, geography, economy, and people of Puerto Rico"--Provided by publisher.
Includes bibliographical references and index.
ISBN-13: 978-0-7614-2218-1
ISBN-10: 0-7614-2218-8
1. Puerto Rico--Juvenile literature. I. Title.
F1958.3.B56 2007
972.95--dc22

2006034087

Photo research by Candlepants, Inc.

Cover photo: Allana Wesley White / Corbis

Back cover illustration: The license plate shows Puerto Rico's postal abbreviation, followed by the year it became a commonwealth.

The photographs in this book are used by permission and through the courtesy of: *Photo Researchers Inc.:* Angelina Lax, 4 (top); John
Dunning, 4 (middle), 19 (bottom); Dante Fenolio, 5 (bottom); Adam Jones, 18 (bottom); Farrell Grehan, 19 (top); David A. Hardy, 35
(bottom); Charles D. Winters, 72 (bottom). *Corbis:* Wolfgang Kaehler, 4 (bottom), 39; Jeffery L. Rotman, 5 (top); Lynda Richardson, 5
(middle); Tom Bean, 9; Tony Arruza, 13; Kevin Fleming, 14; , 23, 29; Jeremy Horner, 25; Stephanie Maze, 33, 61; Bettmann, 35 (top), 48
(bottom), 55, 57; Thais Liorca/epa, 49 (top); David Bergman, 49 (bottom); Reuters, 65; Bob Krist, 69, 73 (middle); Visuals Unlimited, 72
(middle);. *Getty Images:* Jean du Boisberranger, 11; Andrea Pistolesi, 17; , 20; AFP, 49 (middle); John Neubauer, 51. *The Image Works:*
Topham, 16; Tony Savino, 66. *Minden Pictures:* Jean-Paul Ferrero/Auscape, 18 (top); Jim Brandenburg, 18 (middle); SA Team/Foto
Natura, 19 (middle). *New York Public Library:* Humanities and Social Sciences Library, Print Collection, Miriam and Ira D. Wallach Division
of Art, Prints and Photographs, 27. *Library of Congress:* 28, 48 (middle). *Super Stock:* StockByte, 36; SuperStock Inc., 43; age fotostock, 72
(top); Buck Miller, 73 (top). *Index Stock:* HIRB, 44; R. Stuart Cummings, 46; Wendell Metzen, 52; Steve Dunwell, 70; Sarah Putnam, 71.
Envision: Deborah Klesenski, 45. *Magnum Photos:* David Alan Harvey, 47. *Colección Museo de Historia, Antropología y Arte, Universidad de
Puerto Rico:* Francisco Oller y Cestero, Self Portrait ,1889-1892 oil on wood23 5/8" x 17 1/2", 48 (top). *Art Resource, NY:* Smithsonian
Museum of American Art, Washington DC, 50; Smithsonian Museum of American Art, Washington DC, 73 (bottom).

Series design by Anahid Hamparian

Printed in Malaysia

1   3   5   6   4   2

Contents

A Quick Look at Puerto Rico

Nickname: Isle of Enchantment

Capital: San Juan

Population: 3,927,188 (2006 estimate)

Officially Became a Commonwealth: 1952

Flower: Puerto Rican Hibiscus

The flower of the maga tree is a giant red hibiscus-like blossom. All year round, its branches are covered with shiny green leaves. The tree produces both berries and flowers at the same time. The wood of the maga tree is highly prized and used in making musical instruments and furniture.

Bird: Puerto Rican Spindalis

The Puerto Rican Spindalis lives in forests and near plantations, where it feasts on fruits and berries. The male bird has green and yellow markings, with a black-and-white striped head. The female has fainter markings.

Tree: Silk Cotton Tree

The Silk Cotton Tree, or ceiba, grows rapidly, reaching heights of 80 feet or more. White or pink flowers bloom on the bare stems. The fruit is a pod filled with seeds and a cotton-like fiber. The trunk of the tree was once used by native Taino people to craft giant dugout canoes. Ceiba seeds are processed to make cooking oil and soap.

Fish: Parrotfish

The parrotfish was given its name because its mouth resembles a parrot's beak and its scales are bright shades of red, yellow, green, and blue. The mouth of a parrotfish is filled with tiny teeth which it uses to scrape off and feed on algae and other organisms that cling to rocks and coral. Parrotfish range in length from 8 inches to nearly 5 feet. They live in warm shallow water and sleep at night hidden between rocks.

Mammal: Mongoose

In 1877, sugarcane growers brought the mongoose from India to control rats that fed on sugarcane. Mongooses range in length from 10 to 25 inches and can weigh from 1 pound to 30 pounds. These long, brownish gray mammals are successful predators due to their quick climbing and running. Their varied diet of rats, frogs, insects, snakes, birds, and fruit has contributed to an explosion of their numbers in Puerto Rico. They are now considered pests. Even as pests, they have an appealing habit of stretching out their long bodies to sunbathe in the morning.

Amphibian: Coqui

The coqui (pronounced "ko-KEE") is a tiny tree frog that lives throughout the island. At night, coquis climb trees while the male frogs noisily chirp "ko-KEE, ko-KEE." Some forests are home to 10,000 coquis per acre, and their chirping can be deafening. Unlike most frogs, coquis hatch as miniature frogs and not as tadpoles.

Isle of Enchantment

Nineteenth-century Puerto Rican poet José Gautier Benítez called his homeland *un jardín encantado*, which means "an enchanted garden." In his day, Puerto Rico was a sleepy, semitropical island bursting with exotic trees, flowers, fruits, birds, and fish. Today, much has changed. The island now bustles with modern activities. Yet, as gardens bloom, seas sparkle, and rainforests shine, Puerto Ricans are still proud to call their home an "isle of enchantment."

Seas, Mountains, and More

Puerto Rico consists of a main island and several smaller islands, covering an area of 3,515 square miles. Puerto Rico is the most easterly part of an island chain called the Greater Antilles. The main island of Puerto Rico is almost rectangular in shape and measures 111 miles east to west and 36 miles north to south.

Puerto Rico's Borders
North: Atlantic Ocean
South: Caribbean Sea
East: Caribbean Sea
West: Mona Passage

7

By itself, that island is often called "Puerto Rico." But Vieques, Culebra, and several small islets lie to the east of the main island and Mona Island. Other smaller islets lie to the west. Together, these islands form the Puerto Rican commonwealth, a self-governing unit tied to the United States. All the islands of the commonwealth lie more than 1,000 miles southeast of Miami, Florida, 500 miles north of Venezuela in South America, and 80 miles east of the Dominican Republic.

Although Puerto Rico is small in size—just slightly larger than Rhode Island and Delaware combined—it has a wide and colorful variety of plants and animals. There are many types of terrain—from ocean beaches to mountains—and a range of weather patterns. Puerto Rico is divided east to west across its center by high mountains called the Central Cordillera. The island's highest peak, Cerro de Punta, which rises to 4,389 feet, is located there. Nearly fifty rivers run off the mountains toward the sea, many flowing through green and fertile valleys.

The Caribbean Islands, also known as the West Indies, are the largest island group in the world (2,800 square miles). They are divided into three smaller groups: the Greater Antilles, Lesser Antilles, and the Bahamas.

Thanks to winds from the Atlantic Ocean that blow frequent rainstorms ashore, the northeastern part of the main island is especially lush and green. A mountain range called the Sierra de Luquillo rises there. Its highest peak is called El Yunque. This same name, El Yunque, is also given to Puerto Rico's tropical rainforest. That forest is part of the Caribbean National Forest and is the only tropical rainforest in the United States national forest system. El Yunque is dense with giant ferns, orchids, mahogany trees, and bamboo—fascinating plants not found on the United States mainland.

By contrast, the landscape of northwestern Puerto Rico is unlike the northeastern region. Many of its rivers run underground. One of them, Rio Camuy, is the third largest underground river in the world.

A tiny shrimp-like fish, called *Alaweckelia gurneei,* lives among the creatures dwelling in the Rio Camuy or along the river's pitch-dark caves. It is colorless and totally blind.

Much of the land in the northwest is made of limestone. Over time, the rivers, wind, and rainfall have eroded the limestone into dramatic caverns, caves, trenches, and towering cone-shaped hills. This type of geographic area is known as karst.

Tropical rainforests once covered the hills and valleys where farmers now grow coffee beans and other crops.

Weather affects each side of the island of Puerto Rico differently. Like many islands, Puerto Rico has a windier, stormier side, called the *windward* side. The calmer protected side, is called the *leeward* side. Northern Puerto Rico is the windward part of the island. It receives nearly twice the rainfall as the southern, leeward side of the island. The southwestern part is particularly dry. Cacti and other plants that grow under dry conditions thrive in this region. Here, in the dry season of December to April, leaves fall from many of the trees.

For many people, the most popular places in Puerto Rico are the soft-sand coastal beaches that encircle the island. Palm trees, pineapples, citrus trees, and other tropical plants grow throughout the nearby coastal plains. Lagoons, which are salt and freshwater ponds that lie separated from the sea by sandbars or reefs, dot the northern shoreline. So do mangrove trees, which thrive along lagoons. Puerto Rico also has coral reefs. Coral reefs are living structures made up of the external skeletons of tiny animals called corals bound together by calcium and other deposits. Coral reefs provide a rich habitat for sea life along the south and west coastlines.

Of the outer islands, Vieques, is the largest and most populated. It is green and hilly with wide, sandy beaches. Culebra and Mona islands also have wide beaches, but both are quite dry, featuring rocks, cliffs, and cacti.

Climate

Puerto Rico lies in an area of the world known as the tropics. This zone stretches in a band around the earth at its equator. The tropics receive the same amount of daylight in the winter and in the summer because the sun stays in the same position directly over the equator every day. The tropics can be quite hot.

Six main islands and several smaller ones make Puerto Rico a paradise for beachcombers and sunbathers.

Isle of Enchantment

However, since Puerto Rico faces the Atlantic Ocean, where cooling ocean breezes blow, Puerto Rico does not have a true tropical climate. Instead, it has a climate called semitropical, or subtropical. Year round, Puerto Rico's temperatures barely change. The coolest days average around 73 degrees Fahrenheit, and the warmest days average 82 degrees. Coastal areas are warmer than the mountain regions.

Puerto Ricans are quick to point out that barely a day goes by without sunshine. This is true for most areas. However, the northern coast of the island receives frequent rain brought on by steady winds that travel across the Atlantic. Storm clouds push against the mountains and release their rain daily. Rainfall on El Yunque, for example, averages 180 inches a year. But in the crowded coastal areas, annual rainfall is 70 inches in the north and 37 inches in the south. November through April are the drier, slightly cooler months. May through October are the rainy months, during which time the average temperatures are a few degrees warmer.

Although Puerto Rico's climate is generally warm and pleasant, sometimes weather conditions can turn dangerous. This occurs most often during the hurricane season. According to the United States National Weather Service, this season lasts from June 1 to November 30. Hurricanes are intense tropical storms that produce heavy rains and wind speeds of at least 74 miles per hour. Weather experts have said that hurricanes are likely to strike Puerto Rico only once every thirty years. But in recent years, they have been much more frequent.

In 1989, Hurricane Hugo, a record-breaking storm, struck the island with 124-mph winds and left 30,000 people homeless. In 2004, Hurricane Jeanne churned slowly across the island, dumping nearly 24 inches of rain in one day. This hurricane left behind massive mudslides, floods, fallen trees, and power failures.

In 1998, Hurricane Georges destroyed crops, flattened houses, uprooted trees, and washed away bridges.

Island Creatures

Bats, manatees, humpback whales, and dolphins are the only native wild mammals in the region. Few other mammals are native to Puerto Rico. Most of the mammals living in the wild today first arrived on the islands by flying, floating, or swimming from nearby lands. Humans brought other mammals to the island. Mongooses thrive in the forests but are not native to the islands. Early settlers brought mongooses to control rats and snakes—also brought to the island by accident. Rhesus monkeys live on a small, unpopulated Puerto Rican islet. Originally they were brought from India for use in medical research. On the island of Mona, pigs and goats run wild, abandoned by farmers who used to live there.

Herds of wild horses roam free on Vieques. Spanish explorers introduced horses to the islands centuries ago.

Many reptiles and amphibians flourish in Puerto Rico. There are several types of snakes, though none are poisonous, not even the largest snake, the Puerto Rican boa. Lizards, such as anoles and geckos, lurk everywhere—in forests, beaches, and cities. They range in size from the tiny Monito gecko at a mere two inches, to the Mona Island rock iguana, which can grow to four feet. The rarest of Puerto Rico's reptiles are sea turtles. These creatures live most of their life in the open sea. They come ashore only to lay their eggs in the sand. Sea turtles have been hunted for their meat, eggs, or shells. They are considered endangered all over the world. Sea turtles of Puerto Rico include the hawksbill, leatherback, loggerhead, and green turtle. Sixteen different types of frogs live in Puerto Rico. The one most Puerto Ricans are familiar with is the coqui, a brownish frog which sings its distinctive song all night long.

Marine life is abundant in the waters around Puerto Rico. Some areas of the ocean are very deep, while others are shallow and contain coral reefs. Corals need warm, clear, shallow water to survive. They also need wave action from nearby beaches and shallows to wash in food. Coral reefs provide an environment for lots of other marine life. In the coral reefs around Puerto Rico, you can find sponges, sea anemones, octopi, lobsters, conches, angelfish, parrotfish, red snappers, tuna, and dolphins. Mosquito Bay on Vieques is known for its dinoflagellates, which are tiny organisms that live in the world's oceans. At night, the creatures emit an eerie light, causing the water in the bay to glow.

When Puerto Ricans want to say they are proud of their heritage, many use the expression, "I am as Puerto Rican as a coqui!"

Insects and spiders thrive in Puerto Rico. There are more than 200 species of spiders, many of which are harmless. But some carry strong venom, including the black widow, tarantula, and a wolf spider that eats frogs and lizards. There are also about 5,000 species of insects. Mosquitoes, flies, and termites are the most common. Other insects include grasshoppers, dragonflies, beetles, and butterflies.

Many of the more than 250 species of birds feast on the plentiful insects in Puerto Rico. The Guánica Dry Forest on the main island is host to several different migratory birds such as egrets, herons, ibises, and todies, as well as native birds such as the Puerto Rican lizard-eating cuckoo and the Puerto Rican nightjar. Along the coast, sea birds gather. They include grebes, tropic birds, pelicans, terns, boobies, bitterns, ducks, plovers, laughing gulls, and frigate birds. In the forests live hummingbirds, falcons, hawks, screech owls, tanagers, canaries, parakeets, mockingbirds, and doves.

El Yunque forest is one of the most diverse environments in the world, with more than 240 types of trees, 150 types of ferns, and 50 varieties of orchids. Moreover, El Yunque is Puerto Rico's

Environmentalists and the governments of the United States and Puerto Rico are working together to preserve the unique habitat of the El Yunque rainforest.

Just an hour away from the bustling port of San Juan, tourists can hike in the El Yunque rainforest or swim and snorkel at nearby beaches.

most treasured natural region and the source of much of the main island's fresh water. So environmentalists and concerned citizens are working to preserve this remarkable rainforest. They do not want to see it developed—turned into cropland or pasture for grazing animals.

Will these efforts be enough to save the rainforest and the rare Puerto Rican parrots that live there? For now, many citizens, scientists, and government officials are doing all they can. It is an environmental challenge worthy of the "isle of enchantment."

Plants & Animals

Ghost-Faced Bat

Bats are the most common mammals in Puerto Rico. One kind of bat, the ghost-faced bat, is small and reddish-brown, with unusual folds of skin across its face. It hangs by two legs and lives in caves. At sunset, the animal leaves its cave and feeds on insects, capturing them while flying.

Mangrove

Mangrove trees grow in salty wetlands along coast-lines. The trees filter salt from the water and deposit the extra salt into their shiny green leaves. Mangroves breathe oxygen through their roots. Their extensive root system gives shelter to small fish, shellfish, and crocodiles. As the roots thicken and collect soil around them, mangroves protect shorelines from damage due to floods, tides, and storms.

Rhinoceros Iguana

The rhinoceros iguana is a large lizard of the iguana family. Adults are 2 to 4 feet in length and weigh about 20 pounds. They are named for the horn-like scales on their noses. They live in dry forests near the sea. The animals are cold-blooded, so they stay warm by sunning themselves on rocks. Young iguanas are meat eaters, but adults eat mostly fruits, leaves, and berries.

Puerto Rican Parrot

The Puerto Rican parrot, with its large head and brilliant green and blue feathers, is one of the rarest creatures on earth. Once plentiful, these parrots now number fewer than fifty in the wild. The birds have become endangered mostly because of hunting and destruction of their native forest habitat. Environmentalists are working to raise parrots in captivity and release them into the wild to increase their numbers.

Leatherback Sea Turtle

The leatherback sea turtle is the world's largest turtle. It also dives the deepest and stays under water the longest. Unlike other turtles, the leatherback has a rubbery shell. It lays its eggs in the sand of open beaches. Like all sea turtles, leatherbacks are endangered worldwide. They are often caught in fish nets and drown. They also are disturbed by passing boats, and some choke on floating plastic garbage.

Puerto Rican Lizard Cuckoo

The Puerto Rican Lizard Cuckoo is found only in Puerto Rico, living in the island's forests, woodlands, and plantation fields. The cuckoos are colorful birds with long tails and curved bills. They are secretive and move slowly, flying in a straight line while looking for prey. The island's many lizards are their preferred food. The cuckoo can imitate many sounds it hears.

2 From the Beginning

Over many centuries, people from all over the world have landed on Puerto Rico's shores. Most historians agree that people first arrived on Puerto Rico and the islands of the Caribbean much later than on the nearby continents of North and South America. Experts believe it was around 1000 BCE that the first group, called the Arawaks, fled South America when warrior tribes, called the Caribs, chased them northward. Other groups may have floated on rafts from the area that is now the state of Florida. These earliest people disappeared without leaving much behind to tell their story. However, by 1000 CE, another group of Arawak-speaking people, the Tainos, had made the sea journey to the islands from the Orinoco and Amazon river regions of South America.

The Tainos had their own name for what is now Puerto Rico. They called their land *Borinquen*, after a god they believed to be their creator. The Tainos were peaceful. They were also expert sailors, fishermen, and woodworkers who, with stone tools, carved seaworthy dugout boats from whole *ceiba* trees.

Music and dancing have been an important part of life in Puerto Rico for hundreds of years.

The Tainos built well-planned villages. Chiefs, called *caciques,* lived in rectangular straw houses, while workers lived in round huts. The Tainos' buildings all faced a common area called a *batey,* where ceremonial dances and games were held. For food, the Tainos fished and hunted birds, iguanas, and sea turtles. To add to their food supply, they farmed crops, such as maize (corn), beans, squash, sweet potatoes, pineapples, and peppers. The Tainos also grew cotton and wove its fibers into cloth as well nets and sleeping hammocks. Both men and women wore decorations of paint on their bodies, as well as shell bracelets, and jewelry in the form of gold earrings, nose rings, and necklaces.

The English word "canoe" comes for the Taino word "canoa."

Enter the Europeans

In 1493, the Italian-born sea captain Christopher Columbus sailed from Spain to claim lands in the New World that he had visited on his first voyage in 1492. When he arrived on the island of Borinquen, he estimated that there were 50,000 Tainos living there.

To the Tainos, Columbus and his men, with their light skin and beards, appeared unlike anyone they had ever seen. They greeted the newcomers with friendliness and awe. Columbus, however, was not interested in making friends. He was looking for land and wealth for Spain. He gave the island a Spanish name, *San Juan Bautista,* or simply San Juan (which is Spanish for Saint John the Baptist, a Christian saint). Columbus and his men were greedy for the treasures of the Tainos and soon forced them to mine the island for gold.

Carved stone walls surrounded game courts, where the Taino played a sport using a rubber ball.

Sixteen years later, in 1509, Spain appointed a Spanish explorer, Juan Ponce de Leon, to be the first governor of the area. Ponce de Leon's chief duty was to defend the island against raids by the English, French, and Dutch, as well as Carib tribes from other islands. De Leon established a base near a bay on the northeast side of the island and called it *Puerto Rico,* which is Spanish for "rich port."

Soon, Spanish priests and other settlers arrived. They brought farm animals and supplies. King Ferdinand of Spain demanded that the land on the island be divided into large parcels, which he then gave to Spanish landowners. After claiming all the natives' land, the Spaniards forced the Tainos to work for them. The natives were so convinced that the Spaniards were as powerful as gods, they did whatever the Spanish people ordered. They worked on Spanish farms, constructed buildings, and mined and processed gold.

However, by 1511, a group of Tainos rebelled and killed nearly half the Spaniards on the island. The rebels then fled to the mountains or to neighboring islands. After this revolt, though, the Tainos gradually disappeared from the coastal lowlands. Over the years many of them died from diseases the Europeans had brought to the island and for which the natives had no immunities. In just a few decades, the Tainos' way of life was destroyed.

Once the Tainos were gone, the gold ran out on the island, too. The Spaniards looked for other ways to create wealth. In 1518, Spain gave the Spanish people living on the island permission to import slaves from Africa. With the labor of African slaves, the Spanish were able to develop large farming operations, called plantations. Their most profitable crop was sugarcane. They grew the tall, grasslike plants and extracted and refined the sugar from them. They shipped the refined sugar to Europe where it was a prized import. San Juan became a valuable shipping port and a place of power from which Spain could manage its interests and its other lands in the New World.

In 1589, Spanish engineers began building forts to protect Puerto Rico from Spain's enemies. The largest fort was El Morro. Several times, the British and the Dutch attacked Puerto Rico from the sea. Usually, Spain was successful in defending its colony. But in 1598, a British duke and his soldiers took over El Morro and occupied it for five months before sickness overtook them. And later, in 1625, the Dutch attacked San Juan by land and burned the city to the ground. The Spanish settlers rebuilt their city and improved their forts.

From the late sixteenth century to the eighteenth century, Spain did not get along with its European neighbors. That distracted the country from paying much attention to its colony in Puerto Rico. Mostly, the island was used as a port for Spanish ships that traded goods between Spain and its New World colonies. However, the people of Puerto Rico were forbidden to trade with any other country but Spain.

The fort of El Morro once protected early settlers from invaders. Today, visitors can tour the fort's dungeons, towers, and tunnels at this World Heritage Site.

As Spain's troubles grew in Europe, fewer ships entered Puerto Rican harbors, and the island's economy began to fall apart.

In 1755, military clashes began in what is now called the Seven Years' War. Battles took place around the world and involved Spain, France, Great Britain, and other European countries. Many of the battles spread to the Caribbean. Planters and small-time Puerto Rican farmers, called *jíbaros,* took advantage of Spain's lack of attention. The farmers began planting crops for themselves, not just sugarcane for Spain. They grew such things as fruits, vegetables, coffee, and tobacco so they could sell them for profit. Farmers, businessmen, and government officials began to trade openly with other countries. This illegal trade activity, called smuggling, became widespread on the island. Because of all this trade, the Puerto Rican economy improved.

While the American colonies fought for independence from Britain in the American Revolutionary War, Britain barred trading ships from entering any of its ports in the colonies. But Puerto Rico, belonging to Spain, was a safe place for these ships to hide. While anchored in San Juan harbor, the colonies' ship captains smuggled in slaves and food, then traded them for coffee, tobacco, and molasses from Puerto Rico.

By the nineteenth century, many Puerto Ricans referred to themselves as Creoles. This term once described people of Spanish descent born in Puerto Rico. But it had also come to mean people who were a mixture of the island's cultures—Spanish, African, and Taino. In the 1860s, tensions grew between the Creoles and the Spaniards who still controlled the government, most commercial activities, and the military. Despite ending slavery and making some reforms, Creoles began to demand more rights.

Upper-class life in 1860 San Juan was a mix of military and civilian customs that newcomers brought from Spain, Great Britain, and the United States.

The United States Comes Ashore

In 1898, the United States and Spain fought each other in a war called the Spanish-American War. On July 25, 1898, United States troops invaded the southern shore of Puerto Rico. About three months later, on October 18, Puerto Rico came under American military rule. On December 10, 1898, Spain and the United States signed Treaty of Paris of 1898. This treaty awarded Puerto Rico to the United States.

A civil government replaced the military government in Puerto Rico on May 1, 1900. The United States president, William McKinley, appointed politicians to serve as governor, cabinet members, and members of a house of delegates, similar to a senate. The American congress approved each person. The Puerto Rican government then elected thirty-five local people to serve in the smaller house of delegates.

But Puerto Ricans resented this arrangement. It felt like another return to colonial rule with yet another foreign government controlling the country.

To protest the presence of the United States on the island, local representatives to the government refused to pass any laws in 1909. But on March 2, 1917, United States President Woodrow Wilson signed the Jones Act. This law gave Puerto Ricans the right to United States citizenship. It also gave Puerto Ricans some limited personal and civil rights. These included the right to elect some members of their government and to enlist in the United States military.

United States General John Brooke was Puerto Rico's first appointed governor, but citizens soon demanded the right to elect their own non-military leaders.

One month later, the United States entered World War I, and 18,000 Puerto Ricans signed up to serve in the United States Armed Forces.

In the first part of the twentieth century, under the rule of the United States, the Puerto Rican economy had problems. Many Puerto Ricans were poor and made a difficult living on small scraps of land. Sugarcane plantation owners, businessmen, and politicians from the United States held such control over the land that people used the phrase "King Sugar" to describe the wealthy landowners' power. They grew just one crop, sugarcane, and they made a lot of money doing so. This left little land for the Puerto Rican people to grow their own crops.

Finally, in 1920, a Puerto Rican writer named Luis Muñoz Marin, who had been studying in the United States, returned to his country with a desire for change. Muñoz Marin went out into the Puerto Rican countryside and talked to the *jíbaros,* the poor farmers. He promised them "bread, land, and liberty." They elected Muñoz Marin into the Puerto Rican Senate. There, Muñoz Marin worked to improve the lives of Puerto Rico's poor people.

But in the 1930s, Puerto Rico's economy again had problems. The demand for sugarcane dropped drastically after farmers on the mainland United States discovered they could make sugar from their own sugar beet crops.

Owners from outside Puerto Rico controlled its farmland for centuries, making it difficult for islanders to own their land and lift themselves from poverty.

Puerto Rico faced more problems than this. Around the same time, hurricanes hit Puerto Rico, destroying homes and businesses. Poor people struggled to feed and house themselves. Even wealthy people were struggling. Many of them lost money in the crash of the stock market in 1929 and in the Great Depression that followed. With so many challenges, tensions between the United States and the Puerto Rican workers grew. Although the people from the United States built roads, bridges, schools, dams, and hospitals in Puerto Rico, they also angered Puerto Ricans. For example, they declared English as the official language of the island when most of the Puerto Ricans spoke Spanish. Officials also changed the island's currency to the United States dollar, rather than the Puerto Rican peso.

The lives of Puerto Ricans did not begin to improve until the 1940s. By then, Muñoz Marin and the Democratic Populists Party that supported him had more representatives in the government. Their group voted together and gained more power. They pushed for changes, such as bringing clean water and electricity to villages that were a long distance from the island's towns. They encouraged businesses to hire Puerto Rican workers and persuaded United States lawmakers to allow the Puerto Rican people to elect their own governor.

When the United States entered World War II in 1941, 53,000 Puerto Rican men and women served in the military overseas. Puerto Rico became a key military post for the United States, which established army, navy, and air force bases on the main island and on the smaller islands, Culebra and Vieques. The bases provided more employment opportunities for people and helped to attract new industries to the island.

United States military bases have provided jobs and training for many Puerto Ricans, though today that military presence is decreasing.

In 1942, Muñoz Marin and his followers developed a program called Operation Bootstrap. The program called for many changes. Under this program, Puerto Rico became recognized as a "free associated state," or commonwealth. (This was officially stated in Puerto Rico's constitution in 1952.) This meant that Puerto Ricans would not only remain citizens of the United States, they would have more independence. They did not have to pay federal income taxes and could vote for their own government officials. They could not, however, vote for a United States president, nor could their representative in Washington, D.C., vote in the United States congress. Puerto Ricans would continue to use United States currency but could now have their own national flag and national anthem.

Operation Bootstrap encouraged Puerto Ricans to move to the United States mainland in search of better jobs and educational opportunities. The island was becoming crowded, and more than a million people moved north, mainly to New York. Operation Bootstrap also took advantage of the tax benefits in Puerto Rico. The commonwealth invited manufacturers and other industries, including tourist businesses, to move to Puerto Rico and to use local people to fill the new jobs. Overall, the program was an enormous economic success.

In 1948, Muñoz Marin became the first freely elected governor of the commonwealth. Along with improving the economy, he worked to improve healthcare, education, and housing for all people. In the 1950s and 1960s, many United States manufacturers, especially drug companies and textile manufacturers, began to do business in Puerto Rico. Tourism also grew. Because the local families were making more money, their children were able to attend colleges and universities.

All these new changes began to make Puerto Rico the "showpiece" of the Caribbean region.

Yet, some people remained dissatisfied. In 1967, a vote was held to determine whether or not Puerto Rico should remain a commonwealth, become a state, or seek independence as a nation. The vote was 60 percent in favor of remaining a commonwealth, 39 percent in favor of statehood, and only 1 percent in favor of becoming an independent nation. So Puerto Rico remained a commonwealth of the United States.

The debate continues. Today, there are three major political parties, New Progressive, Popular Democratic, and the Puerto Rican Independence Party. Each has a different stand on the question of statehood, nation, or commonwealth.

The Road Ahead

Although most Puerto Rican citizens would agree that the military bases and the factories have improved the economic life of their island, many would also say that these things have also caused serious problems. In recent years, the tax benefits of Operation Bootstrap have become less valuable to manufacturers from the United States. Many factories have laid off workers, cut jobs, or closed. Unemployment is very high. Factories and military bases have also polluted many natural areas on the island. During the 1970s to 1980s, the military built up its presence in Puerto Rico, which has added to tensions in recent years.

There are mixed opinions about the outlook for Puerto Rico's future. Because of the issues of pollution and the loss of businesses and industries, some experts believe the future looks poor. High unemployment, crowded cities, sickness, and poverty are major problems. However, Puerto Ricans are also wealthier, healthier, and better educated than other Caribbean citizens. Some people believe that there is new hope for the island. Sugarcane plantations are no longer a way of life. Farmers are specializing in other crops to export, such as coffee and other tropical foods. The tourism industry is also thriving. United States citizens living in cold, northern states can travel easily to the island for a vacation without needing to carry a passport, learn a new language, or exchange foreign money. Nearly all cruise ships sailing in the Caribbean stop in San Juan harbor.

As citizens work to clean and restore beaches, rivers, and forests, and as new businesses are formed based on tourism, specialty crops, and safer manufacturing processes, there is every reason to believe that the future of Puerto Rico holds great promise.

Important Dates

600 to 1200 Ancestors of Taino and Carib Indians migrate to the islands by dugout canoe from South America.

1200 to 1500 Taino villagers fish and raise crops.

1493 Christopher Columbus lands on the island during his second voyage to the Americas.

1508 Spanish explorer Juan Ponce de Leon establishes the first European settlement.

1518 The first Africans are brought to Puerto Rico to work as slaves.

1521 The island is named Puerto Rico, and San Juan is proclaimed the capital.

Ponce de Leon

1625 Dutch sailors destroy San Juan.

1736 Coffee-growing is introduced to the island and becomes a major export.

1873 African slaves are freed.

1898 The United States declares war on Spain for control of the Caribbean.

1899 Spain gives Puerto Rico to the United States in the Treaty of Paris.

1917 United States President Woodrow Wilson signs the Jones Act, granting United States citizenship to Puerto Ricans.

1946 United States President Harry S. Truman appoints the first Puerto Rican governor, Jesús T. Piñeiro.

1947 "Operation Bootstrap" begins, bringing new industries to Puerto Rico.

1952 Puerto Rico becomes a commonwealth of the United States.

1961 The Arecibo Observatory is established.

1983 The United Nations declares "El Morro" in San Juan a World Heritage Site.

Arecibo Observatory

1998 Hurricane Georges strikes the island with 120-mph winds.

2003 The United States Navy withdraws its base from the island of Vieques.

3 The People

When compared with most of the states in the United States, the commonwealth of Puerto Rico is small in size. However, it is densely populated, with 1,100 persons living in each square mile. That makes it more crowded than any state. Approximately 3.9 million people live on the islands of Puerto Rico, and about 2.7 million Puerto Ricans have moved to the United States. But no matter where they live, or where they were born, Puerto Ricans are proud of their culture and the rich traditions of the "Isla del Encanto."

More Puerto Ricans live in New York City than in San Juan. Those who live or have lived in New York City are known as "Nuyoricans."

Creole Culture

Puerto Rican society is diverse. Many people are descendants of the native Taino people, the Africans, or the Spaniards. Other groups that have contributed to Puerto Rican diversity have included the French from Haiti and Louisiana, Irish and Scottish farmers, Chinese workers who came to build roads, Italian and German immigrants, and Dominican refugees.

Many Puerto Ricans honor their heritage and history by performing traditional dances.

Over the years, Puerto Ricans have blended many cultures to create one Creole culture that shapes all parts of island life: language, religion, art, music, dance, food, celebrations, recreation, and more.

Language and Religion

Because it ruled the island for 400 years, Spain has had the strongest influence on Puerto Rico. By contrast, the United States has ruled Puerto Rico for just over a hundred years. Though Spanish and English are the official languages, more Puerto Ricans speak Spanish than English. Spanish is the language used in public schools, and English is taught as a foreign language. Only about 15 percent of the people speak, write, and read English fluently. However, the everyday Spanish spoken by most people is often influenced by English words.

The Spaniards also introduced their Catholic religion to the island. Today, 85 percent of the people worship as Roman Catholics. Others are of Protestant or Jewish faith. However, many people also follow a religion known as *Santería*, a blend of African, Taino, and Catholic spiritual beliefs and practices.

The Arts

Through the centuries, the island's unique culture has inspired Puerto Rican artists to create remarkable paintings, murals, crafts, and sculptures. The earliest well-known artist was an eighteenth-century painter named José Campeche, the son of a freed slave. Campeche painted religious scenes, as did the European artists of his time, but he used bright, tropical colors.

Many of the craft traditions have roots in the older cultures of the Puerto Ricans' ancestors. Skills for these crafts have been passed from one generation to the next. Since the sixteenth century, whole families of artisans have carved wooden statues called *santos*. Although santos are figures showing Catholic saints, African and Taino craftsmen also carved statues of their gods. The artisans of each Puerto Rican culture influenced each other, creating this unique art form.

Another Puerto Rican novelty is the masked vejigante character. Vejigantes represent evil spirits from an old Spanish legend. So when Puerto Rican artists combined this idea with the African mask-making skills and the Spanish tradition of wearing costumes in carnival celebrations, these traditions blended in a vejigante character. The masks have brightly painted horns, snouts, and devilish expressions. Vejigantes are the highlight of any festival.

A type of lace called *mundillo* is another Puerto Rican handmade item. Only artisans in Spain and Puerto Rico know how to make it. The town of Isabella holds a Puerto Rican Weaving Festival each year to celebrate this rare, 500-year-old craft.

Loiza and Ponce are two cities especially known for their vejigante masks.

Making a *Vejigante* Mask

Historians believe Tainos, Africans, and Spaniards who originally settled Puerto Rico's islands made masks for their festivals. The tradition continues today.

What You Need

A balloon large enough to blow up to the size of your head
5 or 6 sheets of newspapers
Ruler with a metal edge
A small bucket (or large plastic tub) and a
    stirring stick
Large mixing bowl
Plastic or Saran wrap
1 bottle of white glue (4-ounce size)
Water
Masking tape or double-sided clear tape
Styrofoam "peanuts," cut-up egg cartons, sponges, cardboard, or foil
Acrylic paints in various colors and several paintbrushes
Scissors
A foot-long length of string or a rubber band

Spread two to three layers of newspapers over a work area. From the remaining newspaper sheets, tear several dozen strips approximately 1-inch wide and 8 to 9 inches long. (Tearing against the ruler's edge makes the job easy.) Torn strips stick better than cut ones do. Lay a sheet of plastic wrap across the top of the mixing bowl so that several inches hang down to catch drips. Blow up a balloon and rest it on the plastic wrap over the mixing bowl.

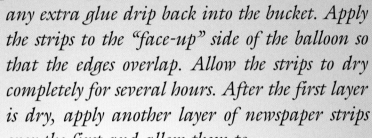

Pour the entire bottle of glue into the bucket. Fill the empty glue bottle twice with cold water—2 bottles of water to 1 bottle of glue—each time pouring and stirring the water into the glue with the stirring stick. The mixture should be very runny.

One by one, dip each newspaper strip into the glue mixture. Let any extra glue drip back into the bucket. Apply the strips to the "face-up" side of the balloon so that the edges overlap. Allow the strips to dry completely for several hours. After the first layer is dry, apply another layer of newspaper strips over the first and allow them to dry for several hours again or overnight.

Use the cardboard, egg cartons, styrofoam, foil, or sponges to make facial features like horns, noses, or bulging eyeballs. Tape down the features with the masking tape.

Paint your mask and allow it to dry completely.

Pop the balloon, and gently pull it away from the mask.

You can trim away any shreds or uneven edges with the scissors. Carefully make a hole on each side of the mask. Tie off a length of string or a long piece of elastic on one side of the mask, then on the other.

Your mask is ready to wear!

Music is another favorite art form in Puerto Rico. "Everything that happens in Puerto Rico is accompanied by music," says one Puerto Rican. "We have no glass in the windows, so you constantly hear music playing, whether you want to or not!"

Puerto Rican musical styles are an exotic blend of Taino, African, and Spanish rhythms and instruments. The Taino danced to long story-songs in ceremonies called *areytos.* They played instruments such as *maracas,* which are dried gourds filled with beans that rattle when shaken. Africans brought drums to Puerto Rico, and the Spanish brought guitars. Puerto Ricans combined all of these influences to create unique musical sounds such as *lamentos,* which are sad ballads, *danzas,* which are formal dances set to classical music with a Caribbean beat, and *bomba y plena,* which are old dances performed to the beat of drums, tambourines, or guitars. Modern music in Puerto Rico also includes the lively and rhythmic *meringue, salsa, reggae,* and Latin pop and jazz. Many Puerto Rican musicians have become famous around the world. Examples include Tito Puente, José Feliciano, Marc Antony, Jennifer Lopez, and Ricky Martin.

Fun and Games

Festivals and celebrations are frequent in Puerto Rico. They vary in custom, but all of them feature live music, dance, costumes, crafts, parades, and traditional foods. Many types of festivals celebrate harvests of crops such as sugar, flowers, coffee beans, and pineapples. Art, craft, and music festivals include the Pablo Casals Festival and the *Bomba y Plena Fiesta.* Political, religious, and ethnic festivals are held throughout the year. Puerto Ricans, being a part of the United States, honor all

Puerto Rico

United States holidays, as well as many of their own national holidays. Some of these national holidays are Puerto Rican Constitution Day, Abolition of Slavery Day, and the birthday of Luis Muñoz Rivera, father of Luis Muñoz Marin.

In addition to all the other festivals, are those in each of the 78 *municipios,* or municipalities, which honor that town's patron saint. *Fiestas patronales,* as they are called, begin with a church service on a Friday, two to twelve days before the saint's birthday. After the religious events end, everyone leaves the church and goes out into the town plaza. Then, for as long as two weeks, musicians play day and night. Food vendors, farmers, and artisans line the plaza, and people dance, shop, and join in parades. Some of the largest and most popular of the saints' festivals are Festival of Saint James (*Fiesta de Santiago Apostol*) and Festival of Saint John the Baptist (*Fiesta de San Juan Bautista*). Other important religious celebrations are Easter week, (*Santa Semana,* which is Spanish for Holy Week) and the Christmas season (*Las Navidades*). During these holidays, many people leave the city and go back home to the countryside, where their families, including grandparents, cousins, aunts, and uncles, gather to celebrate.

Music is a central part of all Puerto Rican celebrations.

Food and Fun

While you can find typical American foods in markets and restaurants throughout the island, Puerto Rico also has its own cuisine, or style of cooking. Food is a major part of every celebration and event. Farmers markets, outdoor food stalls, and open-air cafés all send their tempting aromas into the streets. Fresh fruits such as pineapples, mangoes, coconuts, papayas, and avocados are plentiful.

The word *barbecue* comes from a Taino word. For hundreds of years, Puerto Ricans have cooked zesty meats, such as chicken and pork on outdoor barbecues. Rice and sweet peas (called pigeon peas) are included in a meal almost every day in most households. Plantains are another favorite food. They look similar to bananas, but plantains taste more like sweet potatoes. Cooks prepare plantains either by frying, boiling, or sometimes mashing them. Cooks use a variety of sauces to flavor many meats and vegetables. One example is *sofrito,* which is made from peppers, onions, garlic, tomatoes, and spices,.

"The food isn't spicy in Puerto Rico, it is savory . . . *delicioso!*" report some tourists.

Spices from Puerto Rico, and those imported from around the world, have been part of the island's cuisine for centuries.

Recipe for a Tropical Fruit Smoothie

Puerto Ricans make a variety of drinks with coconut, mango, pineapple, banana, or papaya. On market day, it is fun to stop and sip a cool *batida* (smoothie), or make your own.

Cooking tools you will need:

Cutting board, blender, paring knife, measuring cups and spoons, 2 tall glasses

Ingredients:

1 ripe mango (if unavailable, use
    either a peach, 1/2 cup pineapple
    slices, or 1/2 cup papaya)

1 banana

1/4 cup milk

1/4 cup orange or pineapple juice

6 ice cubes

1 tablespoon honey

1 teaspoon vanilla

Peel the banana and slice it into approximately 2-inch slices. Set aside. With an adult's help, use the paring knife to peel the mango. Slice off 2-inch chunks of fruit and set aside.

   Measure the juice and the milk and pour into the blender. Add the fruit slices. Place the blender lid on tightly. Process the mixture at high speed for about 30 seconds.

   Add an ice cube and process for another 30 seconds. Repeat for each ice cube. Add the honey and vanilla. Replace the lid and process for another 5-10 seconds. Pour the drink into two glasses. Make a toast. Your batida *will be thick, frothy, healthy, and* delicioso!

Outdoor Activities

Puerto Rico's mild climate is good for many outdoor activities. Puerto Ricans enjoy boating, fishing, swimming, surfing, hiking, tennis, and golf all year round. In plazas everywhere, you will find people seated at tables in the shade, playing serious games of dominoes or chess. Other sports passions are baseball, basketball, and boxing. Just as the Taino enjoyed ball games centuries ago, Puerto Rican children and professional players alike play baseball year round. Many major league players from the United States play winter baseball in Puerto Rico. Also, hundreds of talented major league players have come

Snorklers and deep sea divers search for undersea creatures that feed and hide in Puerto Rico's coral beds.

from Puerto Rico, including Roberto Clemente, Juan Gonzalez, Javy Lopez, Sandy Alomar, Bernie Williams, Ivan Rodriguez, José Cruz, and Carlos Delgado.

City and Countryside

During Operation Bootstrap, people began leaving their homes in the countryside (called *el campo* in Spanish) to move to jobs in the cities. Today, the cities are crowded. Suburban sprawl, made up of endless rows of concrete houses, spread outside all the cities. Nearly one third of the Puerto Rican population lives in the San Juan area. People worry that the island is becoming dangerously overcrowded. The crowding can cause serious problems, such as fewer jobs, increased crime rates, and higher cost of living.

However, others are hopeful. "It used to be," says a former San Juan business owner, "that anyone with an education, or anyone who wanted an education, went to the United States and didn't come back." But, in recent years, as the economy in the United States has slowed, many of those islanders who migrated have returned.

Although only about one quarter of the Puerto Rican population lives in the countryside, people remain loyal to the small towns and villages many of them came from. During major holidays, families return to their hometowns. Many mountain villages look much the same as they did a century ago. Throughout the countryside, town plazas are lively centers of action. Some city dwellers are now rethinking their move away from the country. They want to end their dependence on factory jobs and return to farming. During summer's heat, many Puerto Ricans escape to the mountains to relax.

Whether from the city or country, Puerto Ricans love their island. They treasure their rich culture and are proud of its unique place in the world.

Saints' day celebrations like this one on St. Valentine's Day take place on city streets, in the countryside, and at the beach.

Famous Puerto Ricans

Francisco Oller: Artist

Francisco Manuel Oller y Cestero was a nineteenth-century Puerto Rican artist who studied in Europe but returned to his homeland to teach and to paint. Oller painted the island's natural beauty as well as its social problems. His paintings are displayed in museums in Puerto Rico and around the world. They portray a variety of island life, from portraits of governors, to scenes of slaves working on sugar plantations, to scenes of everyday life.

Lola Rodríguez de Tío: Poet

Poet Lola Rodríguez de Tío was born in 1848, and was a descendent of the island's first governor, Juan Ponce de Leon. Rodríguez de Tío became known throughout Latin America for her political poetry. She championed women's rights, abolition of slavery, and independence for Puerto Rico. Throughout the island, schools, buildings, and streets are named in her honor.

Roberto Clemente:
Baseball player

Roberto Clemente was born in Carolina, Puerto Rico, in 1934. He was the first Latino accepted into the Baseball Hall of Fame. At the age of 38, while on a mission bringing supplies to earthquake victims in Nicaragua, Clemente was killed in a plane crash. The Roberto Clemente Award is presented every year to a major league baseball player who combines outstanding skills on the field with charitable work.

Antonia Novello: Physician

Dr. Antonia Novello was born in Fajardo, Puerto Rico, and received her medical degree from the University of Puerto Rico School of Medicine in 1970. After joining the Public Health Service, Dr Novello began working for the National Institutes of Health in the United States. In 1990, she was appointed by President George H. Bush to the post of Surgeon General of the United States. Dr. Novello was the first woman and the first Hispanic to hold that office.

Orlando Figueroa: Space Engineer

As a child in San Juan, Puerto Rico, Orlando Figueroa wanted nothing more than to be a scientist. Excited about space exploration, Figueroa earned a degree in mechanical engineering from the University of Puerto Rico at Mayaguez. Today, Dr. Figueroa is the director of NASA's Mars Exploration Project. Hoping to inspire more young people to enter a career in science, Dr. Figueroa launched a Web site showing photos of NASA's mission to Mars. More than 60 million computer users around the world have logged on.

Ricky Martin: Actor and Musician

Enrique Martin Morales, who uses the stage name Ricky Martin, was born in San Juan on Christmas Eve in 1971. He began performing at age 9. By age 12, he was a member of the Latino pop group Menudo. Later, Martin became a leading man in Broadway theater and a Grammy-winning pop star. He also heads an organization to help abused young people. The United Nations has named Martin a UNICEF Goodwill Ambassador.

Calendar of Events

Las Navidades

The Christmas season, or *Las Navidades,* lasts from early December to January 6, Three Kings' Day *(el Día de Reyes).*

During *Las Navidades,* neighbors gather and go caroling from house to house. On the eve of Three Kings Day, children set out shoeboxes filled with grass. According to legend, three kings riding camels visit each house on that night. After the camels eat the grass, the kings fill the shoe boxes with gifts. The next morning, January 6, children awaken to holiday presents and treats.

Three Kings' Day

Pablo Casals Festival

In 1957, the most famous concert cellist of the time, Pablo Casals, left his Spanish homeland because it was at war. Casals moved to Puerto Rico and founded a major music festival. To this day, the festival attracts classical musicians and music-lovers from around the world.

Carnaval

Carnaval, also known as "Mardi Gras," is the celebration that occurs the week before Lent begins. Lent is a 40-day period of fasting before the Christian holiday of Easter. In cities and towns throughout Puerto Rico, *carnaval* is celebrated with colorful parades, costumes, song, and dance.

San Juan Bautista Day

San Juan Bautista is Spanish for Saint John the Baptist, the patron saint of San Juan. The city's residents enjoy lots of food, song, and dance on June 24, the eve of the holiday. At the stroke of midnight, partygoers line the city's beaches and jump into the ocean backwards, a tradition meant to renew good luck in the year ahead.

Aibonito Flower Festival

The mountain town of Aibonito comes alive at the end of June with a weeklong festival devoted to plants. Fields of roses, lilies, orchids, and other flowers burst forth with color and aroma in the town's *Fiesta de las Flores.* Thousands of visitors come to buy flowers and enjoy crafts, music, dance, and traditional foods.

Fiesta de Santiago Apostol

Each town in Puerto Rico has a festival honoring its patron saint. The town of Loíza was settled by Nigerian slaves in the 1500s and celebrates its African heritage with a festival to the town's patron saint, Saint James. Over several days in July, people pay homage with parades, Afro-Puerto Rican music and dance, traditional foods, and the wearing of coconut shell masks called *vejigantes.*

St. Apostol Day

Hatillo Masks Festival

In December the northwestern town of Hatillo reenacts the biblical story of King Herod. In the legend, the King ordered all baby boys to be killed in order to do away with the threat of baby Jesus and protect Herod's position as King. In Hatillo, masked devil-soldiers in colorful costumes run through the streets looking for children. But it is just a game, and as in all Puerto Rican festivals, there is lively music, dancing, and traditional foods.

MONUMENTO DE LA RECORDACION · MEMORIAL MONUMENT

4 How It Works

Puerto Rico underwent centuries of changing rules and governments before it became a commonwealth of the United States in 1952. Perhaps that status will change again. Meanwhile, its government structure is similar to the local, state, and national governments in the United States.

Levels of Government

The Puerto Rican government is organized into three levels: municipal, commonwealth, and federal. Municipal governments are local. They are made up of a village, town, or city, and its surrounding area called municipalities (*municipios*). Citizens of a municipio elect a mayor and an assembly. All seventy-eight municipios in Puerto Rico have their own coats-of-arms and their own flags. Each coat-of-arms has a Spanish nobleman's crown, which stands for the protection the government gives all its people. Also pictured on the coat-of-arms is a group of three to five castle towers. The number of towers shows if the municipio is a village, town, or city.

The capitol building was a gift to the Puerto Rican people from the government of the United States in 1929.

53

The second tier of government in Puerto Rico is the commonwealth government. In 1951, the people were asked to approve a constitution the United States prepared for the island, by which all Puerto Ricans would abide. Eighty-one percent of the people voted in favor of the document. Many of the laws and features found in the constitution are similar to those found in the state constitutions of the United States. For example, there are three branches of government and a bill of rights. In the commonwealth, voters elect a governor, who is the highest level executive of the government. The governor, in turn, has the important role of appointing all judges and other executive office holders. Citizens also elect senators and members of a house of representatives. The commonwealth has its own flag and its own national anthem.

As a free associated state, Puerto Rico relies on the United States to provide many services it provides states on the mainland, such as postal service, communications systems, military defense, and customs and immigration enforcement, and foreign relations. Puerto Rico belongs to the federal court system of the United States and is part of the First Circuit Court. Puerto Ricans are United States citizens and are free to come and go to the mainland of the United States without having to get a visa, or special permission, which is usually required when a person travels abroad.

When living on the island, Puerto Ricans do not pay United States federal income tax (a tax that comes out of a person's salary.) However, they do pay federal Social Security tax. They can collect Social Security and some other federal income payments from the United States. (Social Security benefits help when you are retired or unable to work.)

Branches of Government

Executive The governor is the powerful head of the executive branch. The governor appoints all judges and all department heads. He or she signs bills into law and can also refuse to sign bills. This refusal is called a veto. The governor is elected to a four-year term, and there is no limit to how many times he or she can be re-elected.

Legislative The legislative branch, or congress, is usually made up of twenty-seven senators and fifty-one members of the house of representatives. All members of congress are elected to four-year terms. If voters elect members from one political party to hold more than two-thirds of the seats in either the house or the senate, then extra seats are added to the congress and assigned to members of the minority parties. Nine seats may be added to the senate and up to seventeen may be added to the house.

Judicial The judicial branch is a system of courts made up of the supreme court, court of appeals, and the court of first instance. The governor appoints all judges, with approval of the senate. The highest court, the supreme court, is made up of seven justices. The court of appeals hears challenges to rulings made in other courts. The court of first instance is divided into two sections: superior court and municipal court. Superior courts hear the major civil and criminal trial cases. Municipal courts make decisions on small claims and lesser crimes.

Puerto Ricans can enlist in the military of the United States and are included in any military draft, when it is in effect. Citizens can vote in the primary elections of the two major political parties in the United States, the Democrats and the Republicans. But they cannot vote for the United States president. They do elect one representative to the United States house of representatives. However, that representative is called an "at-large" member and is not allowed a vote in congress.

Puerto Rico has its own Olympic teams and competes as an independent nation in events, such as basketball, boxing, diving, tennis, and figure skating.

Luis Muñoz Marin, governor of Puerto Rico from 1949 to 1964, introduced ideas that drew many new businesses to the commonwealth.

Puerto Ricans have been debating one major political issue for a long time. Do they want to be a state like all the other fifty states in the United States? Do they want to remain a commonwealth connected to the mainland? Or do they want to be a truly independent country? Everyone has an opinion. Each of Puerto Rico's three major political parties has a different point of view.

In 1967, 1981, 1993, and 1998, voters attempted to resolve this issue. The first three times, Puerto Ricans voted to keep the status of commonwealth. But some people were unhappy with that.

In the 1967 vote, for example, many Puerto Ricans resented that their young men were drafted into the military and sent to war in Vietnam, while those same soldiers and their families were not allowed to vote for or against the president who sent them.

The New Progressive Party believes that Puerto Rico should become the fifty-first state. Supporters of statehood want their votes to count on matters affecting the United States. If Puerto Rico were to become the fifty-first state, then citizens would be able to vote for the United States president, two congressional senators, and up to eight congressional representatives. Leaders on this issue also say that the island would receive additional government funds from the United States.

On the other hand, the Puerto Rican Independence Party says the island has been no more than a colony and should now become an independent nation. Followers of the Puerto Rican Independence Party believe that a new constitution, one that Puerto Ricans write independently of the United States, would better protect their Hispanic language and culture.

The Puerto Rican National Guard arrested rebels during their 1950 fight for independence from the United States.

They say that if they win independence, Puerto Rico would be able to manage its own money, its radio and television broadcasts, immigration laws, trade with other countries, and most importantly, its own defense. Many in Puerto Rico dislike the United States military controlling their land, waters, and air space.

A third view comes from the Popular Democratic Party, which wants the commonwealth status. Commonwealth supporters believe that the tax benefits, trade partnership, and protection of the United States military, as well as citizenship rights, offer the best of both worlds. Puerto Ricans are wealthier and better educated than any of their Caribbean neighbors. People credit the commonwealth association with the United States for their prosperity.

In 1998, when a vote for "Commonwealth, Independence, or Statehood?" was placed before the people, the pro-statehood party was in power. When they designed the election ballots they called the commonwealth choice a "territorial" commonwealth. People knew that such a commonwealth carries fewer rights than an "associated free state" commonwealth. The pro-statehood party believed that by making the choice sound worse than it was, people would not vote for any form of commonwealth and instead vote for statehood. But, there was another choice on the ballot labeled "none of the above." The Popular Democratic Party, which supported the commonwealth status, urged voters to select "None of the Above," meaning nothing would change. So, in the 1998 vote, the majority of Puerto Ricans voted for "none of the above." In 2005, the Puerto Rican governor, Anibal Acevedo Vila, vowed to continue the debate with another vote to "put it in the hands of the people."

How a Bill Becomes a Law

Like the United States and most of its fifty state governments, Puerto Rico has two houses of congress: a senate and a house of representatives. Each of these is sometimes called a "house." The chief duty of their members, also called legislators, is to create laws. A legislator can suggest a law bill in either the house of representatives or the senate. One exception is that all tax-related laws must begin in the house of representatives. When a legislator has an idea for a bill, the bill must be printed out and given to a committee to decide if it is a good idea. Each bill is assigned a number. House bills begin with "HR" and senate bills begin with "S." No bill can have more than one subject.

Committees within each house focus on particular topics such as education, agriculture, natural resources, health, transportation, and taxes. During committee meetings, members discuss the bills and listen to people who have come to talk about them. If a committee approves a bill, it is presented to the other members. The other legislators then debate the bill and suggest changes. Once the committee finalizes the wording of the bill, it is put to a vote within the house where it was created. If the bill receives a majority of the votes, it is sent to the other house. When the bill is received in the other house, it is assigned a new number and goes through much the same process of committee discussion and voting.

If the bill passes in both houses, it is presented to the governor. The governor can sign the bill, making it law. Or the governor may object to the bill and return it to congress with suggestions for changes. The governor can refuse to sign the bill altogether. This action is called a veto. If the bill is vetoed, it can still pass into law if two-thirds of the people in both houses still vote in favor of it.

Here is how the process worked in the 1990s. In 1902, the American government decided that English, along with Spanish, would be an official language of Puerto Rico. Since that time, English has been taught in schools and used to communicate in the tourist business, in international trade, and in federal government relations. However, most Puerto Ricans speak and write in Spanish.

In 1991, legislators in the Puerto Rican House of Representatives passed a bill declaring Spanish the only official language of the commonwealth. The bill was sent to the Senate, where it also passed. It was later signed by the governor, Rafael Hernández Colón. However, in 1993, a new governor, Pedro Rosselló signed a bill reinstating English as one of two official languages.

In the ongoing debate over Puerto Rico's political status, language again became an issue in 2003. This time, the senate passed a bill declaring Spanish the only official language.

The Governor's mansion, called *La Fortaleza,* was built in 1540 as a fortress to guard the entrance to the San Juan harbor. It is the oldest continuously used executive mansion in the Western hemisphere.

The debate about Puerto Rico's possible statehood or existing commonwealth status continues in public demonstrations.

Puerto Rico

As one lawmaker explained, "The official language of a country is the one with which the government communicates with its people and vice versa." Eighty percent of the population spoke Spanish. When the bill was sent to the house, members there also agreed with the bill. However, the governor, Sila Maria Calderón, refused to sign the bill. Today, both English and Spanish remain the official languages of Puerto Rico.

To find out more about Puerto Rico's legislature go to this Web site http://www.oslpr.org/english

5 Making a Living

The Taino were Puerto Rico's first farmers. They grew a healthy variety of crops and fed themselves with ease. When the Spanish colonized the island and took over the farmland, they planted just a few money-making crops to trade with Europe. Among the first plantation crops were sugarcane and coffee. Farmers grew sugarcane in the valleys, and planted coffee beans in the mountains.

As one citizen recounts, "Puerto Rico grows the finest coffee in the world. All the houses of kings once ordered coffee from the island growers. Every year, the best of the crop was delivered to the Pope." The United States was also an important importer.

At the height of Puerto Rico's success as a coffee exporter, two severe hurricanes destroyed the big plantations. It took years for the farms to recover. When they did, the United States had begun buying coffee from Brazil. Because of this, the coffee plantations declined. The United States continued to import huge quantities of sugarcane until the 1940s, after which the sugarcane plantations failed. Only a few remain today due to competition from sugar beet farming in the United States and

Modern gourmet coffee drinkers around the world have developed a taste for strong-flavored Puerto Rican coffee beans, which are a growing part of the economy again.

around the world. However, coffee farmers are growing and exporting coffee again.

Little land is available for agriculture in Puerto Rico. Only 3 percent of all the island's workers are involved in farming. But many people feel the need to develop more farms. They are worried that the island relies too heavily on the United States for food. Rice, for example, is very important in all Puerto Rican kitchens, yet Puerto Rico grows very little rice. Instead, it imports tons of the grain from the United States each year.

"Just forty miles away in the Dominican Republic, there are rice paddies everywhere," says one man.

Recently, the government has tried to encourage farming. In the western region, farmers grow fruits, avocados, rice, and native root vegetables. Livestock farmers raise cows and chickens for meat, milk, and eggs. Citizens can buy these fresh home-grown foods at weekly farmers' markets held in the central plazas of cities and towns. Along with coffee, Puerto Rican farmers also export bananas, plantains, coconuts, and pineapples.

Plantains, a staple of the Puerto Rican diet, are also exported to the United States and other countries.

Natural Resources

Puerto Rico is a small island group with limited natural resources. Many of its forests have been cut to make way for plantations and housing. Today, few trees are left to harvest for lumber. Some forests, however, are being replanted.

Fishing was once a very typical way to earn a living. But it is no longer a major source of income. Many people who fish commercially also hold other jobs. Commercial fishermen catch about 3 million pounds of fish a year and other seafood that includes tuna, lobster, shrimp, crab, and conch. About 15 percent of that is consumed in Puerto Rico and the rest exported. Fish farming is a growing business, however. Fish farmers raise bass and catfish in freshwater pens and sell them to local shops and restaurants.

Precious metals such as gold, copper, iron, and silver were once mined on the island, but the mines have closed. Today, most of the minerals mined, such as sand, gravel, lime, clay, and stone, are used to build houses and roads.

Transportation

"It used to take half a day to get to Mayaguez. Now, there are highways everywhere, and it takes twenty minutes," comments a man from San Germán.

In the past two decades, roads and highways have been extensively improved. There are more than 14 thousand miles of roads and nearly 2 million cars. Streets are often packed with the despised *tapones,* or traffic jams.

"Oh," says one shopkeeper, "you should see the cars thread their way through Old San Juan. They go one after the other all day and on into the night!" To help relieve some of the congestion, a mass transportation system that serves

San Juan and nearby cities, called the *Tren Urbano*, or Urban Train, opened to the public in 2005.

While cars, buses, and trains move people around the islands, airplanes and boats move people to and from the islands. The large international airport in San Juan is named after Luis Muñoz Marin. Smaller airports serve the rest of the Caribbean region. Water taxis and ferry boats bring passengers and supplies to the islands of Culebra and Vieques. San Juan and Ponce are the Caribbean's chief ports for container ships and cruise ships. They are among the busiest ports in the world.

Manufacturing

Over 10 percent of the labor force in Puerto Rico is employed in manufacturing jobs. In the 1940s, people left their traditional fishing and farming jobs and went to the cities to work in the new factories launched by Operation Bootstrap. The United States government encouraged development in Operation Bootstrap by giving companies from the United States and other countries special tax breaks, loans, and research help if they would set up factories in Puerto Rico. Many large corporations are there to this day, including General Electric, Hewlett-Packard, Johnson & Johnson, Pfizer, and Procter & Gamble. Puerto Rican factory employees make clothing, medicines, chemicals, electronics, and many other useful products.

Deep in the Cordillero mountain range, the Arecibo Observatory is the site of the world's largest single-dish radio telescope. There, scientists and astronomers from around the world map galaxies and study pulsars and other phenomena in the skies.

The special tax laws have changed over the years and are less beneficial to the companies. As a result, many of them are reducing the number of employees they hire in Puerto Rico and moving their factories to countries where labor is cheaper. Yet Puerto Rico has an educated workforce, so jobs in high-technology, chemicals, and medical products are still a very important part of the island's economy. Many of the most commonly prescribed medicines in the United States are manufactured in Puerto Rico.

Puerto Rico has a favorable business climate and an educated population that is ideal for the manufacture of medicines.

Service Jobs

Nearly 30 percent of Puerto Rico's labor force has service jobs. Service workers include hotel clerks, restaurant workers, health care workers, lawyers, shopkeepers, and bankers. The government employs over 20 percent of Puerto Rico's workers, such as teachers, postal carriers, and firefighters.

The numerous military bases around the islands employ thousands more people. The United States Navy recently left its operations on Vieques and decided to close its largest naval base in Puerto Rico, Roosevelt Roads. As a result, 2,500 people lost their jobs in 2005. With so much change happening in the labor force, many people in Puerto Rico are turning to the tourism business for jobs. They believe that tourism is an important key to economic growth. Each year, more than 4 million visitors vacation in Puerto Rico, many from the United States.

Service workers make up a large portion of the workforce in Puerto Rico.

Although the tourists' money is welcome, some people believe the many new hotels, restaurants, and cruise ships add to crowding on the islands and strain resources.

One form of tourism that protects the environment while still providing jobs is eco-tourism. Eco-tourists are people who enjoy visiting a place and studying the natural areas. They stay in small inns or in people's houses and eat at local restaurants. Eco-tourists come to Puerto Rico to kayak in the lagoons, hike in the rainforest, birdwatch, spelunk in caves, snorkel in coral reefs, and study other natural features. The Puerto Rican eco-tourism industry is working with scientists, environmentalists, local business people, government officials, and others to pre-serve and protect their land's tropical beauty. Possessing such a special place in the world, Puerto Ricans have a bounty that they are proud to share.

Schoolchildren in Puerto Rico join environmentalists and eco-tourists in helping the endangered leatherback turtle.

Products & Resources

Coffee

In the 1800s, Puerto Rico coffee plantations were among the most important in the world. But coffee growing slumped for many decades in the twentieth century. Now, with renewed interest in Puerto Rican coffee, today's farmers plant it high in the mountains, 3000 feet above sea level. Their coffee tastes rich and sweet and is prized by gourmet coffee drinkers everywhere. Coffee is Puerto Rico's most valuable agricultural crop.

Medication

Of the twenty best-selling drugs in the world, Puerto Rico produces sixteen. Nineteen major pharmaceutical (drug) companies operate on the island, including Eli Lilly, Merck, and Johnson & Johnson. Combined, they run more than sixty laboratories and factories and employ 11 percent of the island's workers.

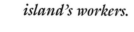

Salt Mining

The oldest industry on the island, begun by the Spanish in the sixteenth century, is salt mining. The largest mine is in Cabo Rojo, where both table salt for foods and mineral salts for bathing are found.

Tourism

Nearly 5 million tourists visit Puerto Rico each year and spend close to 3 billion dollars there. Many arrive via cruise ship and pass through the Caribbean region's largest port, San Juan. Luxury hotels, year-round warm weather, and sandy beaches are major attractions.

Textiles

Fine needlework such as lacemaking is a centuries-old skill of many generations of Puerto Rican women. The craft became popular in the United States, too, when influential Americans such as Mrs. Thomas Edison and President Franklin Delano Roosevelt and his wife, Eleanor, purchased traditional Puerto Rican textiles. Later, clothing manufacturers from the United States set up factories. Today clothing manufacture is a leading industry, and the craft of lace-making remains popular.

Puerto Rican Santos

Since the sixteenth century, Puerto Rican artists have carved wooden Catholic saints, called santos, for display in people's homes. Until the early twentieth century, there were few churches in Puerto Rico, so communities prayed together at family altars decorated with santos carvings. Modern carvers today continue the tradition. Art collectors, folk-art museums, and galleries around the world feature antique and modern santos in their collections.

The flag of the commonwealth was adopted in 1952. It is based on a design created years earlier by patriot and poet Lola Rodríguez de Tío, in 1854. It resembles the Cuban flag, with the colors reversed. Five stripes; three red and two white, represent the rights of citizens, freedom, and the three branches of government. A white star inside a blue triangle represents the commonwealth. The flag was adopted in 1952.

In the sixteenth century, the king of Spain presented a seal to Puerto Rico. Figures from that seal are part of the island's present seal. A lamb, represents peace and brotherhood. The letters F and I stand for Ferdinand and Isabella, the king and queen of Spain at the time. Old symbols of royalty, such as the Towers of Castile, the Lions of Leon, the Crosses of Jerusalem, and various Spanish family flags also appear.

Puerto Rico

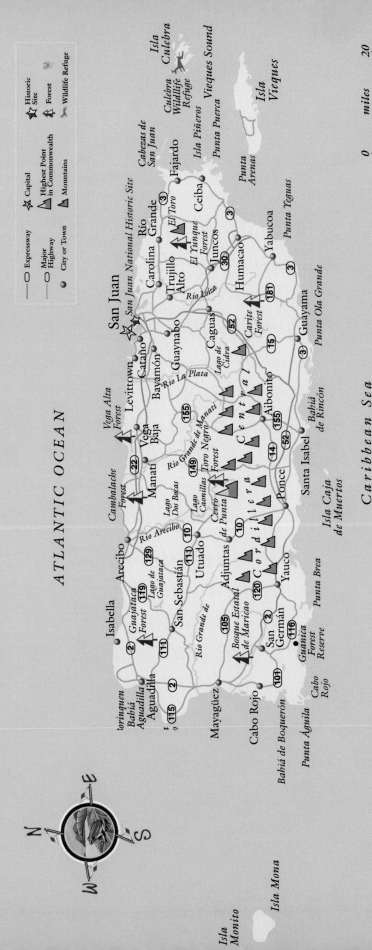

La Borinqueña

Puerto Rico

Official Song

More About Puerto Rico

Books About the Commonwealth

Heinrichs, Ann. *Puerto Rico.* Minneapolis, MI: Compass Point Books, 2004.

Of Special Interest

Delacre, Lulu. *Vejigante Masquerader.* New York: Scholastic Inc., 1993.

Ford, Carin T. *Roberto Clemente: Baseball Legend.* Berkeley Heights, NJ: Enslow Publishers, 2005.

Mohr, Nicholasa. *The Song of el Coqui and Other Tales of Puerto Rico.* New York: Viking, 1995.

Montes, Marisa. *Juan Bobo Goes to Work: A Puerto Rican Folktale.* New York: Morrow Junior Books, 2000.

Taus-Bolstad, Stacy. *Puerto Ricans in America.* Minneapolis, MI: Lerner Publishing Group, 2005.

Web Sites

Links to Puerto Rican history, culture, politics, environment, and people:
http://welcome.topuertorico.org

El Yunque Forest Web site:
http://www.fs.fed.us/r8/caribbean

About the Author

Ruth Bjorklund lives on Bainbridge Island, near Seattle, Washington. On cold, rainy days, she and her husband and their two children daydream of Puerto Rico's sunny skies and warm, sandy beaches.

Index

Page numbers in **boldface** are illustrations.